Goudhurst to Tenterden

IN OLD PHOTOGRAPHS

Cranbrook, *c.* 1860. This must be one of the earliest photographs of the area in existence and shows an old house in Stone Street.

Goudhurst to Tenterden

IN OLD PHOTOGRAPHS

Collected by AYLWIN GUILMANT

Alan Sutton Publishing Limited
Phoenix Mill · Far Thrupp
Stroud· Gloucestershire

ALAN
SUTTON

First Published 1992

**British Library Cataloguing
in Publication Data**

Guilmant, Aylwin
  Goudhurst to Tenterden in Old Photographs
  I. Title
  942.2392

ISBN 0–86299–686–4

Typeset in 9/10 Sabon
Typesetting and origination by
Alan Sutton Publishing Limited.
Printed in Great Britain by
WBC Print Ltd, Bridgend.

Contents

Introduction

The areas covered by this book can be linked in a variety of ways, one of the most significant being the iron workings of the Weald. Broadly speaking this was the region near the Kent and Sussex border which carried a dense forest on the clay soil. As a consequence it had been under-populated for centuries. The iron workings commenced during the time of the Roman occupation and reached their zenith in the sixteenth century. Iron works flourished in villages such as Cranbrook, Hawkhurst, Goudhurst and Biddenden, to name but a few. From about the 1660s the industry declined as the scarcity of timber coincided with the importation of iron from the continent. Nothing now remains of the iron industry in this area, but its existence is still indicated by names such as 'Furnace Road,' or 'Hammer Stream' which remind us today that this was once 'the black country' of England.

'Domesday Book' records that the Weald (the last area to be settled by the Saxons) was valuable as pasture for swine in small partially cleared areas which were called 'dens'. Tenterden, for example, was the swine-pasture of the Minister-in-Thanet. Much of the Wealden forest was owned by monasteries or by manors, which were eventually handed over to the king's Norman kinsmen.

In 1499 Tenterden (and its neighbouring port of Smallhythe, which was to become an important ship building centre) received its Charter of Incorporation as a 'limb' of Rye and as a consequence became a member of the Confederation of the Cinque Ports. As one of two 'Antient Towns' linked to the Cinque Ports, Rye had been unable to meet its obligation through a series of disastrous French raids. It consequently turned to its nearby and wealthy neighbour, Tenterden, for assistance. Tenterden's maritime association was gradually lost during the fifteenth and sixteenth centuries, due in some measure to the changing coastline. Despite this it remained an important distribution centre for a wide variety of goods, including the famed 'Kentish broadcloth'.

Edward III was responsible for inviting foreign workmen to settle in Kent, partially in order to strengthen the English cloth industry. Many of the towns of the Weald were involved in cloth-making but, being somewhat coarse, the cloth was suitable only for local needs and not for export.

Many of these foreign workmen, some Flemish, settled in and around Cranbrook. This was a prime centre for cloth-making, the area being rich in the two commodities necessary for finishing the cloth – fuller's earth and sufficient water power to drive the hammers of the fulling mills. Cranbrook was also close to Romney Marsh, a rich grazing area for sheep, although the wool from these flocks was considered to be somewhat inferior to that from flocks in other parts of the country.

The cloth-making industry flourished in many of the places mentioned in this book, but much of the work was carried on in small isolated units. Processes such as spinning and carding often took place in the homes of the workforce. Weaving (for which the Flemish were renowned) was carried on in the master cloth-worker's 'hall' where finished goods were also stored. The industry was very labour intensive and Jessup in his *History of Kent* states that the output from the Weald of finished cloth amounted to between 11,000 and 12,000 pieces a year. The total value would have amounted to somewhere in the region of £150,000, a vast sum of money in the reign of Elizabeth I.

Regulations were slowly introduced including the stipulation of the width of Kentish broadcloth, and further restrictions were placed on the producers regarding the standard of the finished work. At the height of its prosperity in about 1580, Cranbrook supported a population of some 3,000, while that of the county town of Maidstone was little more than 2,000. Certain rivalries broke out between the clothiers and the iron-workers over the dwindling supplies of timber; the consumption of fuel for the latter was enormous, and this in some ways contributed to the decline of the cloth-making industries in the area.

Kentish agriculture gained importance from the sixteenth century onwards and ultimately became one of the most important sources of wealth. Many early writers such as Camden and Lambarde commented on the agricultural prosperity found in the county. Particular mention was made of the number of new farmhouses erected during this period, when many people in Kent gained their livelihood from agriculture or associated occupations. Cherry and apple orchards increased in number while the introduction of the vine was an added bonus.

Some of the smaller towns covered by this book had flourishing markets; cattle and sheep together with local agricultural produce were regularly despatched to other parts of the country. This distribution was aided by the many branch lines of the railways which opened during the latter years of the nineteenth century. The market at Goudhurst operated well into this century and might have continued but for the Second World War and the axing of its direct link with the main line railway in the 1960s. Before the coming of the railway the roads in the Weald were almost impassable to wheeled traffic during the winter months, although some improvement had been effected with the earlier turn-piking of certain roads.

During the nineteenth century the population in many villages rose, peaking in the middle of the century, although this was not the case in many villages in the western part of the Weald. In Biddenden the population fell over a period of 120 years, according to Jessup, while that of Benenden, over the same period, increased by eight; both these villages had seen a rise during the middle of the century. Today these villages are well sought after places in which to live, despite the fact that many have lost their local bus service and can no longer be reached by rail.

The closing years of Queen Victoria's reign saw these small market towns becoming completely self-sufficient with many small industries and plants. Both Cranbrook and Tenterden had their own breweries and became important centres catering for the needs of the surrounding area.

Unfortunately the twentieth century has seen the closure of various industries, breweries, rail connections and the loss of the area's markets. In their place, however, other industries are set to boom. Today this particular area of the Weald is becoming very popular with tourists both from home and abroad. Many independent schools are to be found in the large houses, once home to private individuals, and as a consequence many visiting parents patronize the small inns and hotels in the neighbourhood thus continuing the prosperity of one of the most attractive and scenic areas of south-east England.

SECTION ONE

Agriculture and Hops

It has been impossible to identify the site of this photograph taken of a way of life from a bygone age. The furrows are being planted with seed by a man with a bag, sometimes called a seed-lip, slung across his shoulders. The team of women in the background are clearing the ground of stones and other such debris. Kent is not only renowned for its hops but also for its cherry and apple orchards and even today excursions are run to view the blossom.

Although some farms used teams of horses, oxen were much in demand on the heavy clay soils of the Weald. Here a team of oxen is working with a typical Kent farm wagon of the period, around 1870. The man on the wagon is Ambrose Bull.

A team working in a field, *c.* 1885. It is believed that the man on horseback is the farmer.

A vegetable garden, *c*. 1890. A garden like this was probably a valuable asset to a labouring man as it provided fruit and vegetables to supplement a poor diet and a meagre wage. In many instances the garden would have been worked entirely by the housewife, assisted by various children.

Hop-pickers in a Kent hop-garden, *c.* 1905.

Mrs Maybourne senior and her family in the hop-garden at Hartley. Her son Jack is on the right of the picture.

Smith's hop-garden, *c.* 1910. Almost in the centre of Cranbrook and close to the tannery, it is believed that part of this former garden is now used as a car park.

London families often came hop-picking, spending up to a month in the country. All members, whatever their age, were expected to do their fair share of the hard work. The railway companies laid on special 'Hopper' trains and local farmers conveyed the pickers to and from the gardens in their wagons. Conditions in the gardens were far from ideal with inadequate huts without sanitation or water. The local people also worked in the gardens, and the school registers always showed a sharp fall in the number of pupils present during the month of September.

Hops were often grown as a cash-crop by local farmers, but many of the larger gardens in Kent were owned by the breweries. Most of the pickers came from the villages of East Sussex or from London. The latter sometimes caused problems for the locals due to the differing life-styles.

A wagon loaded with hop-pokes standing in front of a group of oast-houses, c. 1900. Today many of these hop-oasts have either been demolished or converted into comfortable homes.

Stringing the hop-garden, c. 1910. This was a specialized occupation and the skill was often handed down from father to son. The work itself was difficult, and considerable practice was necessary to master handling the stilts required, especially over the rough ground in the gardens. This method was more relevant to the area around Maidstone than in the gardens along the Kent and Sussex border.

Hop-pickers, homeward bound. Londoners being conveyed to the nearest railway station by farm wagon.

Hop demonstration, 9 May 1908. Many demonstrations like this took place in London and the south-east against the import of foreign hops to the detriment of the local industry. This demonstration at Tenterden in the heart of the hop-growing country took the form of decorated farm wagons with appropriate slogans. The growing of hops in Kent and Sussex has continued to decrease and most of the distinctive hop-oasts have now been demolished or serve other purposes.

Hops were grown in great profusion in many areas of Kent and along the Sussex borders. The gardens gave employment both to the local labour force and to itinerant workers. The hop-poke seen here towers over three of the men.

Hop-pressing in operation. Hops have always played an important part in the economy of Kent. In 1880 the county of Kent produced 42,977 tons – far more than anywhere else. Thirty years later, however, this figure had halved.

SECTION TWO

Goudhurst

The recumbent figures in the church of St Mary depict Sir Alexander and Dame Constance of Culpeper who lived at Bedgbury in the sixteenth century. Queen Elizabeth I stayed with them on her way to Rye and afterwards knighted Sir Alexander. This monument is particularly interesting as it is carved out of wood rather than the more usual stone.

Goudhurst Church

Goudhurst church, *c*. 1920. The church stands in an elevated position and dominates the village. The tower was popular with early photographers as a vantage point from which to photograph the surrounding area. A description of the village in 1884 described it as 'standing boldly out on an eminence in the most beautifully undulating portion of the Weald'. While the church was described as an 'imposing edifice' the original tower was struck by lightning and the present one was built in the seventeenth century.

Goudhurst church from an early engraving, *c*. 1800. Unfortunately it has been impossible to decipher the name of the artist.

The view from Goudhurst church tower, looking across the Weald. The village stands nearly 500 ft above sea-level and it has always been stated that the air is pure and bracing due to this elevated position. From the church tower it was claimed that it was possible to count sixty-eight church towers and spires. The county of Kent is said to be 'the garden of England'; claims have been made that Goudhurst must therefore be 'the garden of Kent.'

Parish hall, Goudhurst. Goudhurst is a splendid village, built on a hill and dominated by its square-towered church, in the lush Kent countryside famed for its orchards and hop-gardens. It is said that a tunnel runs from The Star and Eagle Hotel to the church and was used as a hide-out by the notorious band of smugglers known as The Hawkhurst Gang. The gang was led by Richard Kingsmill, who was ultimately sentenced to death for his crimes and hanged in 1796. His name still evokes interest among residents and tourists alike.

Goudhurst village and church, *c.* 1890. The area shown was once the site of the market before it moved first to a setting nearer the pond, and then to its last position beside Hope Mill station.

Goudhurst market, *c.* 1930. The auctioneers were Messrs Hudson, Mills and Smith.

Goudhurst cattle market, c. 1930. Many of the towns and large villages in the Weald had their own markets, some of which were forced to close when the railways were axed in the 1960s. According to Mr Len Pierce, Secretary and Historian of Goudhurst Local History Society, Goudhurst market was originally near the church where there was a market cross until it was removed in 1652. Goudhurst cattle market subsequently moved to an area beyond the pond, and ultimately to a site near the railway station, shown in this photograph. The village also had an annual fair held on 26 August.

Hope Mill station, *c.* 1892. The official opening of Hope Mill station (subsequently renamed Goudhurst) was on 1 October 1892. However, the occasion shown may have been a rehearsal for 'the big day' as the date of the photograph is 12 September 1892. The station was opened to serve both Goudhurst and Lamberhurst. In 1893 the line was extended to Hawkhurst (see p. 62). The station held an important position, opposite Hope Mill, with the cattle market moving to a site nearby. The railway lost much of its passenger traffic with the advent of the motor-bus, and was axed in the 1960s. Many of these local stations were a considerable distance from the village centre.

Hope Mill, Goudhurst, was mentioned in documentation as early as 1516. In 1837 it was rented by James Clementson who worked the windmill at Brenchley. James went into partnership with John Slaughter who had previously been carrying on business at Hope Mill. They traded under the name of Slaughter and Clementson, which became Clementson and Son when Slaughter retired and Edward Clementson, who bought the mill in 1891, came into the family partnership. Hope Mill ceased to work in 1925 and gradually deteriorated until it was bought in the 1970s by Mr and Mrs Julian Hippesley who converted it into a house. Mrs Hippesley subsequently remarried following the early death of her first husband and still occupies the mill.

The mill house was at one time home of the millers at Hope Mill, Goudhurst. Today it is a private home.

Mr Clementson and members of his staff at the corn mill, *c.* 1880. The boy sitting in front is believed to be the miller's son, who subsequently took over the business and carried on his trade of miller until 1925.

The last miller, Mr E. Clementson, measuring out corn in Hope Mill, *c.* 1920. In 1937, twelve years after the mill had closed, the miller's stock-in-trade and farming stock were put up for auction on the instruction of Mr Clementson. Among the items listed were 5 pairs of millstones, 44 ft of shafting, flour scalper, bran scry, 8 sack barrows, hoisting, timber and other chains, scales and weights, stone proving iron, mill slings, maize and cake mills, power chaff cutter, grindstone, shearing machine, turning lathe.

The interior of Hope Mill when in
working order, *c*. 1920.

Fixing a grindstone in position, *c*. 1920.

The weir, Goudhurst.

Local Goudhurst children standing beside the pond some years before it was 'walled-in'.

'Walling-in' the village pond opposite The Vine, one of the old coaching inns. The blacksmith's forge was behind the trees. This wall is still in existence today and may be seen below the level of the road. The area around the pond has long been known as 'The Plain'. In the last century it was a popular meeting-place for the villagers, while the pond was an ideal spot to water horses after the long pull up the hills to Goudhurst.

The High Street, Goudhurst, 1935, decorated with flags and bunting in celebration of the Silver Jubilee of King George V and Queen Mary.

The High Street, looking up the hill, decorated on the occasion of a royal celebration. The patriotism of the general public is very apparent from this picture, with every building displaying flags and bunting. The number of shops suggest that Goudhurst was quite 'self-sufficient' in pre-war days with a wide variety of goods available.

Goudhurst post office, 1935. Many of the local shops vied with each other in decorating their premises on the occasion of the Silver Jubilee of King George V and Queen Mary. The post office, shown here, was no exception.

Postmen outside the post office. Back row, left to right: F.H. Rayner, J.J.A. Turk, E. Lloyd. Front row: W.G. Fishenden, P. Fishenden.

The window of C. Verral's Chemist and Optician, decorated for the coronation of King George VI in 1937. The new king's portrait may be seen on display. It is interesting to note that three of the advertisements relate to cigarettes and a dispenser for the same may be seen on the left of the doorway.

A window-display in C. Verral's chemist shop, c. 1935. Many old photographic plates were found in this shop and these throw a valuable and interesting light on the social history of the area in and around Goudhurst.

Old and young alike enjoyed the celebrations for the Silver Jubilee of King George V in 1935. These were followed two years later by similar activities on the occasion of the coronation of King George VI and his consort, now the Queen Mother. Bunting and flags decorated the streets and the whole village enjoyed fêtes, processions and a wide variety of amusements. The children in this decorated cart represent the countries making up the British Isles attended by the figure of 'John Bull', alias George Sargent. The girls are sisters, the daughters of the local butcher. England was represented by Patricia Burfield, aged 4, her eldest sister Margaret, aged 13, was Scotland, Mavis, aged 9, represented Ireland and Kathleen, aged 11, wore the distinctive costume of the Welsh. The man holding the horse is J. Isted.

Decorated lorries, cars, carts and floats all took part in the Jubilee procession held in Goudhurst, 1935. The one shown here depicts the work of the village blacksmith, who would have been kept very busy in an agricultural centre such as Goudhurst. The elderly man on the right hand side of the photograph is Mr Amos Mercer.

The Jubilee celebrations were very popular with the residents of Goudhurst, young and old alike. Seen here are many of the children who took part in the parade, among them some of the prize-winners.

Goudhurst firemen taking part in the Jubilee procession held in the village. The horses used by the brigade belonged to a local coal merchant and were stabled behind the fire station. It is believed that these stables belonged to the house named 'Pinehurst'. They had a brick floor and stamped on the reverse side of many of the bricks was the date and the words 'Diamond Jubilee', presumably that of Queen Victoria in 1897. These bricks are much prized by the local residents today as a reminder of Goudhurst's past. In 1875 the fire brigade shed was destroyed, ironically by a fire, and in 1877 a new engine-house was built at a cost of £120. It was surmounted by a turret and stood on the site of the Old Manor Pound, where stray animals used to be impounded until claimed, opposite the pond.

Planting coronation trees in 1937. The house in the background, known as 'Maypole', has since been demolished.

It is believed that this group of people were gathered together to hear King George V deliver the first speech to be made on radio. Judging by the number of young people present it was an auspicious occasion.

Local Cubs and Scouts, *c.* 1935. Many of the boys still live in and around Goudhurst today.

Girl Guides and Brownies from Goudhurst. The vicar and a representative from the local Scout and Cub packs are standing towards the back of the group. Over sixty young people belonged to these organizations during the inter-war years.

The Royal and Ancient Order of Buffaloes was obviously an important institution to many local men as this photograph, taken in 1928, testifies. These men were all members of the 'Freedom Lodge' which seemed to cater for all ages.

Goudhurst village band, *c.* 1935. Many of the young men were enthusiastic members, often introducing brothers and other family members to the band.

Hunt's Lane, Goudhurst, *c.* 1920.

The Vine Hotel and Burgess' store early this century. Apart from the absence of traffic and the flock of sheep wandering down the hill, this scene is remarkably unaltered today.

North Road, Goudhurst, *c.* 1890. Many of the small market towns of the Weald were quite self-sufficient and served the surrounding farming community with the necessary services such as forges and wheelwrights. The latter is seen here beside Lindridge's grocers shop, which subsequently became Humphrey's.

Another view of North Road, somewhat later. The grocers shop is now owned by Humphrey.

North Road, looking northwards early this century.

Goudhurst village, *c.* 1890. Previously considered a market town, the village was well served with shops, many of which are still in existence today. Seen here are the premises of Allwork Bros who were grocers, drapers, general outfitters and also sold furniture and bedding.

Looking down High Street, *c.* 1900. Note the early coffee-house on the right of the photograph.

Mr Burfield, poulterer, outside his shop in Goudhurst, *c.* 1935.

Freddie Southan, butcher, outside his shop with a prize-winning beast.

The Burgess store, *c.* 1940, with a window displaying a poster in aid of the Wings Appeal. This shop, originally founded by a member of the Burgess family and still operating under this name today, sells a very wide variety of goods and is a valuable asset to the village of Goudhurst. It is believed that the building was the original home of a Flemish clothier in the sixteenth century. Members of the Burgess family have run this store for over 150 years, one member having nine daughters. The last Burgess was Mr Geoffrey who handed over the business to Mr K.B. Johnson, the present owner and proprietor, who has kept this shop for the past seventeen years. It is believed that in the early days the business consisted mainly of the sale of cattle food and chicken food. A delivery service was offered, the stables being behind this building which goes back to a considerable depth. Today the ivy has been stripped off the building. The elaborate verandah may have been the work of Davis & Leaney in 1889, a well-known building firm which had records dating back to the year 1883. They were responsible for much work in and around Goudhurst.

SECTION THREE

Hawkhurst

The church of St Laurence, Hawkhurst, *c.* 1908. This building was bombed during the Second World War and subsequently rebuilt.

The Eight Bells Hotel, *c.* 1910, with its new entrance porch. Originally called The Six Bells, the name was altered in 1863 when the church peal was increased by two. At present the building is being rebuilt as it suffered a disastrous fire within the last year, when much of it was destroyed.

The old workhouse stands close to St Laurence church. The pond has since been grassed over as it became a general dumping ground for local rubbish. Following the Reform Act of 1834 it was decided that all relief should be given only in the workhouse and it became a grim establishment: men and women were separated; discipline was harsh; diet was inadequate; strict rules were enforced. Many people dreaded the onset of old age as the late nineteenth-century workhouse was looked upon as the last refuge for the rural poor.

Hawkhurst is reputed to be one of the biggest villages in Kent and comprises three parts: The Moor, Highgate and Gills Green. Part of the village may be seen in the distance with the spire of the church of All Saints just discernible on the skyline. Today the village is a popular centre for the many independent schools in and around an area noted in the past for its iron-workings and cloth industry.

The Limes and Moor Side, Hawkhurst, *c.* 1911. Moor Side was formerly Vine Cottage and was built in 1741 by John Brooke, who resided there. At the same time, The Limes was occupied by John Chittenden, a wealthy clothier. Vine Cottage was subsequently owned by Edward Wickens who also owned the local brewery.

This etching by F. Esam, executed in 1806, shows The Queens Hotel, Dunk's almshouses and a windmill just visible in the distance.

This etching of the same date shows Highgate, Hawkhurst, early in the nineteenth century, before the attractive Colonnade was built. The sign for The Royal Oak is plainly visible as is the distinctive bell tower of Dunk's almshouses.

Mr Ebenezer Williams was a well-known figure in Hawkhurst and responsible for many of the photographs taken of the area. He opened The Studio in Cranbrook Road in 1873 and continued in business until 1925. Mr Williams travelled around the countryside on his tricycle. His other interests were singing in the choir at Northgrove chapel and playing the flute with the local orchestral society.

Mr Lewis Waghorn was born in the house with the trellised extension. This was the shop of his father who was the Hawkhurst baker. At the end of the terrace was the grocery store of A.J. Sims.

The Hawkhurst pharmacy at the Colonnade, Highgate, *c.* 1910. Both the pharmacy and the toilet saloon and barbers shop next door were run by A.J. Cray. Standing in the middle of the block was J.W. Edwards' general hardware and implement stores, the proprietor of which may be one of the men standing outside. It is believed that the Colonnade was built in the early nineteenth century by Peter Umander.

The Royal Oak, *c.* 1920. Formerly known as The Commercial Inn, The Royal Oak was originally three sixteenth-century cottages which stood in a commanding position on the London–Rye highway. It ultimately became a posting inn. The high gable extension was added in 1869 and the porch was a subsequent addition. Note the early motor car standing in front of the building.

Highgate, Hawkhurst, *c.* 1925. The war memorial would have been a relatively new addition (see opposite). The motor coach, parked on the right outside The Royal Oak, was part of a regular service between Hawkhurst and Rye.

At one time stage-coaches ran from Hawkhurst to Tunbridge Wells and to Maidstone. This re-enactment of the service is believed to have taken place around 1920.

The Queens Hotel, *c.* 1910. Bying's Tours of 1788 described The Queens Hotel thus: 'In the row of houses stood our inn the Queen's Head of nice aspect; nor did it deceive us for everything was neat and confortable . . . ' It is believed that Queen Elizabeth I visited this inn while on her way to Rye in 1573. Behind The Queens Hotel was a bowling-green which was reputed to be one of the oldest in the country, although sadly this closed in 1976.

The 'local lads' *en route* to fight for 'King and Country' in the First World War. Luke Pantry may be seen in the vehicle holding a parcel.

Looking over Cockshoot Farm from The Meadows. This photograph shows the beautiful countryside around Hawkhurst.

A family group on the front steps of Theobalds, which was later demolished. This picture was taken the day before the son Mr H. Deakin Liley, seen in the centre of the group, lost his life in an aeroplane accident on 12 July 1915. Also in the photograph are Mr and Mrs Henry Liley, who were great benefactors of the village, and Mrs Liley's companion, Miss Littleton.

Hawkhurst Orchestral Society at Theobalds, home of Mr and Mrs Liley in 1908. It is believed that the pianist was Miss Sivyer. Others in the picture include Messrs George Martin, George Sivyer, W.G. Oliver, William Groves and H. Barhan. Mr Ebenezer Williams, Hawkhurst's own photographer, was flautist with this group for a number of years (see p. 49).

Tongswood was considered the 'jewel in the crown' of the many beautiful houses in the area of Hawkhurst. At one time it was occupied by C.E. Gunther; it subsequently became St Ronan's School.

The ballroom at Tongswood was built by Messrs Davis & Son of Hawkhurst for Charles C. Gunther in 1904. It has been claimed that Mr Gunther embarked on this project in order to create employment for local people during a time of great hardship among many of the poorer paid members of the community.

Hawkhurst Rifle Club, *c.* 1910. The club flourished in the years prior to the First World War. In the picture may be seen Messrs Elliot, Scott, Hemsley, Mark Jenner and Sid Gaspar.

Reynold's Farm, Hawkhurst, *c.* 1900. The farm was in the the hands of Alfred Saxby from 1895 until 1912 when William Court took it over, followed by Horace Taylor in 1919. The name 'Reynold's' may have been derived from a family called Reaynaulds, and a monumental inscription gives a date of 1612. There is further reference to William Reynold Yeoman, who died in 1771, and his wife Martha who predeceased him, dying in 1745. Unfortunately it has been impossible to identify the family busily working in the garden.

A family group outside Reynold's Farm. It is believed that the two older ladies could be the mothers of the young couple with their small daughter. Earlier this century extended families were the norm, with members from three generations sharing a home.

This photograph was probably taken at the same time as the previous one. One of the older ladies has donned a coat for a ride in the carriage, as has her young companion.

Two of the several shops in the Colonnade were Frank Williams, stationer, who also had the office for the *Kent and Sussex Post*, and J.E. Bashford, tobacconist and hairdresser (see pp. 50–1).

A donkey carriage outside the Colonnade at Hawkhurst, *c.* 1870. Unfortunately it has been impossible to identify the occupant but he appears to have been a man of wealth and aroused a great deal of curiosity judging by the number of young spectators.

A.H. Kenchington's flour delivery van at Highgate. The van driver was Charley Rootes.

Oxen in the stack yard, *c.* 1890. These cattle are believed to be some of the six-strong team from Conghurst Farm. To drive such a team took a great deal of practice and experience. The only means of enforcing commands was by means of the ox-goad, a thin hazel stick with an iron projection, used in conjunction with a few gutteral phrases such as 'mothawoot', and 'yahaawoot'.

A team of oxen in front of the Colonnade at Hawkhurst, *c.* 1890. These beasts may have been some of the six from Conghurst Farm.

Extending the railway from Hope Mill, Goudhurst to Hawkhurst in 1892–3 involved considerable embanking and cutting due to the hilly nature of the countryside. This line was officially opened in 1893, and was axed in the 1960s. Hall Wood Farm can be seen in the background.

Work on the line from Goudhurst to Hawkhurst, *c.* 1892.

Hawkhurst station, *c.* 1908. The importance of Hawkhurst increased with the opening of the railway station in the last decade of the nineteenth century. Unfortunately the line was axed by Beeching in 1961. According to Mr Lewis Waghorn, Mr Ollie James is driving his 'pair' and was responsible for conveying passengers to The Royal Oak, while Mr Reuben Vidler waits behind with Lockyer's bus. It is interesting to speculate whether a friendly rivalry existed between these two as it was said that both met all 'down' trains.

Mr William Rootes was originally a resident of Goudhurst, where he had run his cycle business. He and his family then moved to Hawkhurst and lived at No. 7 Cranbrook Road from where he operated his business, having a shop window inserted into the premises in order to display his cycles. Mr Rootes senior had two sons, William (Billie) and Reginald (Reg) Rootes, who were responsible for extending the business to include motor cars. They ultimately went into production nationally in association with the Humber Hillman Sunbeam Group. The advertising on the shop windows, however, is for Ford 1 ton trucks, touring cars and Fordson tractors. The Rootes also held the agency for Singer and Arrol Johnston in the early years of the car industry.

Employees of Rootes Motor Works together with two boys, who it is believed are Reginald and William Rootes, enjoying a spin in an early model.

Dunk's Endowed School at Highgate, Hawkhurst, *c.* 1911. A commemorative plaque on the building gives the name of the founder together with the date 1723. The man standing on the left, wearing his apron, is Mr A. Pannett, a local saddler and harness-maker.

Highgate Infants School in 1898. The headmistress is Mrs Warren, wife of Bill Warren, a millwright. Her assistant Miss Jane Watts is seen on the left of the back row. Unfortunately it has been impossible to identify the other two adults, but one may be Miss Marie Moore.

Dunk's Endowed School, Hawkhurst, 1916. When Sir Thomas Dunk endowed this school for boys, the building was flanked by almshouses where elderly residents, three male and three female, lived. According to Hawkhurst historian Lewis Waghorn (back row, second from left), the headmaster was particularly brutal in his treatment of the boys and meted out corporal punishment on a daily basis. Back row, left to right: Eric Hardcastle, Lewis Waghorn, Norman Suter, Eric Reed, Bill Angell, Buster Brown, Roy Allen, Wally Nunns. Second row: A.C. Moore (headmaster), Sid Jenner, Stanley Saxby, Stanley Playfoot, Aubrey Marchant, Bill Baker, Reg Muggeridge, Dick Bird, Ginger Payne. Front row: Lewis Jenner, Cyril Waghorn, Roland Piper, Len Jameson, Bill Clarke, Frank Goodsell, ? Menzies.

A coronation day procession by children of various ages through the village of Hawkhurst during the summer of 1911. Most children on this occasion would have been presented with a souvenir mug and a bun, and those attending school would have been given a half-day holiday. It is interesting to see that everyone in this photograph is wearing a hat. Among the boys is Cyril Waghorn, younger brother of Lewis Waghorn, whose family have lived in the village for almost two centuries.

Planting of the coronation oak at The Moor, Hawkhurst, on 30 December 1911. Two local people have been identified: Mr Hardcastle of New Lodge and Mrs Liley.

Mr Older, millwright, is standing on the left of this photograph wearing his distinctive paper hat which protected his head from sawdust and wood-shavings. Mr Older and his fellow millwrights walked long distances, often rising at 4 a.m., in order to put in a full day's work at the various mills where they carried out repairs, including those at Sandhurst and Cranbrook.

Nightingale windmill was the last working mill in Hawkhurst. Otto Waghorn, great uncle to the local historian Lewis Waghorn, was the miller. The sails, which are set at a precarious angle, came from another mill at Gun Green and were transported by bullock-cart.

One of the most important shops in Hawkhurst was that of E.W. Court at Warwick House. As can be seen, it sold a wide variety of goods and was considered by many of the local inhabitants to be the best drapery store in the area.

The opening of the International Stores must have created some hardship for other shops in the village. The large staff included Sylvia Jamieson (second from left), Marjorie Westor (fourth from left), and Mr Playford on the extreme right. The International Stores always photographed their staff dressed correctly in their white aprons and standing in front of the shop which displayed a wide variety of goods. The stores closed in 1980.

Four Throws post office, grocers and drapers, 1919. The shop was run by a Mr Waters; his assistant, Mr Cogger, is standing in the doorway.

The old post office at Highgate, *c.* 1885. On the porch are notices relating to the post office savings bank and another announcing that it is also the postal telegraph office. The large building on the left was Dr William Milsted Harmer's asylum, Northgrove House, which was destroyed by a disastrous fire on 4 December 1890 with the loss of one life.

Mr Walter Tickner with the Sunday school class from the Baptist chapel, *c.* 1912.

The 'Babies Castle' at Hawkhurst was opened by HRH Princess Mary Adelaide, Duchess of Teck, mother of Princess Mary, later Queen Mary, who accompanied her on this occasion. This home, run by Dr Barnardo's, catered for many blind and partially sighted children and was in continual use for over eighty years until its closure in 1963.

Children and their nurses enjoying the sunshine in the spacious grounds of the 'Babies Castle', *c.* 1920.

SECTION FOUR
Cranbrook

Cranbrook High Street in 1903, looking remarkably similar to the present day; with the increase in traffic, however, few children would be tempted to play in the road. Many of the properties in the town date back to the sixteenth century when Cranbrook was at the height of its prosperity and the centre of the cloth industry. In 1580 the population stood at 3,000 (in excess of Maidstone, the county town). Earlier it had had a thriving iron works and names connected to this industry may be seen throughout the surrounding area.

Looking up the High Street during a period of very heavy snow, c. 1890. Several of the buildings on the left have been demolished this century.

A general view of the High Street at the turn of the century. The figure on the right of the picture is delivering milk from a churn.

An early picture of the High Street, *c.* 1900 (see p. 79).

A procession in the High Street led by the town band, celebrating the coronation of King George V.

Cranbrook High Street, looking east, *c.* 1910. The buildings, although a medley of styles from different periods and built with a wide variety of materials, seem to blend harmoniously together. This portion of the street was mainly residential (see opposite, above).

Cranbrook High Street, looking west, *c.* 1910.

Cranbrook High Street, looking towards the junction with Stone Street, *c.* 1920. Even at this later date many of the shops still favour canvas canopies, although most of the uprights visible in the photograph on page 77 have disappeared.

Beer barrels outside The Old White Lion, now the post office. It has been suggested that, at one time, this building may have been occupied by a cooper.

A print of the Old Broadcloth Manufactory, *c.* 1800. The gable end subsequently became known as The Old Studio and was occupied by members of the 'Cranbrook Colony' of artists.

The Old Studio in the High Street is a fine sixteenth-century timbered house. For many years during the second half of the nineteenth century it was the residence of F.D. Hardy and Thomas Webster, who initiated the 'Cranbrook Colony' of artists. These painters depicted some of the interiors of local houses in their work and used family groups including many children as their models. The portion of the building on the right is identifiable as the former Old Broadcloth Manufactory.

Vestry Hall, Cranbrook, *c.* 1901, with St Dunstan's church in the background. The hall was built in 1859 from the proceeds of the sale of Sissinghurst Castle Farm, which had been used to support the poor of the parish since 1794. It has been used for a variety of purposes during the last hundred years, serving as a magistrates court and a drill hall. During both world wars it was used for the benefit of the troops, as an emergency hospital during the First World War and as a canteen during the second. At one time a market cross stood on the site in front of the hall.

Cranbrook Fire Brigade in 1879 outside the station which, at that time, was situated in Vestry Hall.

A disastrous fire took place at Cranbrook on 25 May 1840. It was reported in various pamphlets of the day including the *Maidstone Journal*. The fire was discovered at 10.30 p.m. in the house of Mr Beezie, who had recently moved there to carry on his trade of upholsterer. The family consisted of Mr Beezie, his wife, three children, two apprentices and two female servants, who all jumped from the upstairs windows in their nightclothes. Mr Siggs, a shoemaker who lived next door, was also evacuated when the flames engulfed the adjoining houses. Two gangs of men, under the direction of the Revds Boys and Davies, Dr Jobson and other gentlemen, volunteered to obtain water from a nearby rivulet and a pond behind the properties. One fire engine was brought by hand from Staplehurst, others came from Hawkhurst and Tenterden, and two hours after the fire was discovered the Norwich and Kent fire office engine arrived from Maidstone. Sparks fell on the surrounding premises, including Mr Judges' bakers shop. Fortunately no lives were lost and by 3 a.m. the following day all danger of the fire spreading was over. Mr Beezie, who had only had his house for a week and was uninsured, lost not only his own possessions, but also some of those belonging to his clients.

This market cross, *c*. 1920, was erected to replace a much earlier one. It no longer stands and it has been said that it was so badly damaged by a London taxi that it had to be removed. The building behind the cross is Vestry Hall.

The 'modern' market cross, *c*. 1910, stood at the junction of the High Street and Stone Street on the site of an earlier one.

Stone Street, looking north. In the foreground two young girls are pushing a mail-cart in which children sat back-to-back. Behind them may be seen the carrier's van of C.A.T. Williams who operated a twice weekly service between Cranbrook and Maidstone.

Stone Street, looking towards the junction with Waterloo Road. The International Stores may be seen on the left hand side and above the clock the sign of E.A. Jervis, draper. The International Stores subsequently moved to a site in the High Street.

Stone Street, *c.* 1900, is narrower and considered by some to be more picturesque than the High Street. In the past Cranbrook was the centre of the Kent hat-making industry and many people were employed in a factory at the back of a shop in this street. Another business carried on in the area was worsted manufacturing and stocking making, with fourteen worsted machines operating, giving employment to a large number of local inhabitants. The George Hotel on the right dates from the early fifteenth century. It was rebuilt and enlarged a few years before the visit of Queen Elizabeth I in 1573 and subsequently refronted in the eighteenth century.

NOTICE.

W. B. TOOTH,

Respectfully informs the Public, that he has taken the

HAT MANUFACTORY

AND TRADE,

heretofore carried on by his Father, and hopes, by strict attention in its various Branches, to merit support.

Cranbrook, March 4th. 1839.

[G. Waters, Printer, Cranbrook.

A notice relating to the hat factory. It is interesting to see that this early announcement was printed by G. Waters, a local printer of Cranbrook.

It is difficult to decide whether this picture held by Cranbrook Museum is a painting or a tinted photograph. It shows Mr W.B. Tooth, the owner of Cranbrook hat factory, at work on one of his products. The many manufacturers of Cranbrook in the nineteenth century continued a tradition which first commenced with the clothiers of the Tudor period.

The hat factory in Tanyard Passage owned by Mr W.B. Tooth. The factory and trade had first been operated by Mr Tooth's father.

Mr William Tarbutt, 1810–93, was one of the earliest historians of Cranbrook, although by trade he was a basket-maker. In 1840–1 he recorded the population of the town as 4,250 and detailed the following trades and occupations followed by the residents: 21 hotels and businesses, 13 boot-makers, 8 bakers, 7 blacksmiths, 6 tailors, 5 wheel-wrights, 4 millers, felmonger, gunsmith and brass engraver, clock-maker, saddler and harness-maker, linen weavers, lace-makers, basket-makers, cabinet-maker, brickworkers, a rope walk, tannery, brewery, candle factory, worsted factory and a hat factory. For many years he lectured on the history of the town.

CRANBROOK.
LITERARY ASSOCIATION.

On Thursday, November 30, 1865,

A PAPER WILL BE READ BY

MR. TARBUTT.

SUBJECT:

DENCE'S SCHOOL

AND
SCHOOLMASTERS,

FROM 1568 TO 1865.

Also some information respecting other Public Endowments under the will of Alexander Dence.

☞Many curious and interesting facts will be brought forward.

Admission, Members, Free. Non-members, 1d.

To commence at half-past 8 o'Clock.

G. Waters & Son, Printers and Bookbinders, Stone Street, Cranbrook.

A notice announcing a lecture to be given by Cranbrook's own historian Mr William Tarbutt on 'Dence's School' and scheduled to take place on 30 November 1865.

Mr Langridge, the last stationmaster at Cranbrook. The line was one of those axed by Beeching in the closures of many of the branch lines in the 1960s.

The old police station in Waterloo Road, built *c.* 1864. It was demolished in 1967. Today only the steps remain and the site is part of Cranbrook School.

Police Constable Watkins, the last mounted policeman in Cranbrook.

George Dadson, 1791–1880, was chief overseer of the Hundred of Cranbrook, an office he held for a number of years, being paid the sum of £300 per annum.

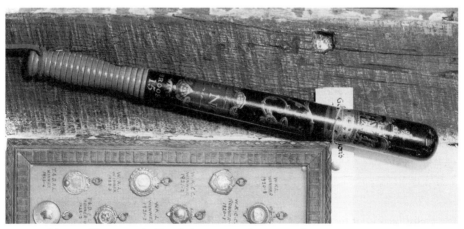

A constable's staff; a sign of office belonging to George Dadson.

The East Kent Regiment, 1902, prior to its departure for South Africa. The regiment included Cranbrook volunteers.

The cyclist section of the East Kent Regiment, 1902. The section was an important body of men, some of whom may have been Cranbrook lads.

Many local banks produced their own notes in the last century. This five-pound note was issued by the Weald of Kent Bank and dated 20 April 1813.

CRANBROOK
PENNY BANK

COMMITTEE.

Mr. T. O. BEEMAN. Mr. DENNETT. Mr. FARRAR.
Mr. GRAY. Mr. TROUGHTON. Mr. TYE.
Mr. WILLIAMS. *Cashier,*---Mr. TATE.

The Cranbrook Penny Bank will be opened on *Tuesday,* May 11th, 1858, at the Residence of Mr. TROUGHTON, when Deposits will be received, subject to the following Rules.

The Office will be opened from Seven till Eight o'Clock every *Tuesday* Evening.

Any amount not less than One Penny will be received.

One week's notice to be given of the withdrawal of all or any part of the Sum deposited, except in *special* cases.

N.B.----Deposit Books will be given to Persons applying within one month from the date of opening : after that date, they will be charged at the rate of one penny each.

A notice relating to Cranbrook Penny Bank, 1858. The Penny Bank first opened in a private house, the residence of Mr Troughton of Cranbrook. The bank continued to operate on similar lines over a number of years.

NOTICE.

The business of the Penny Bank will be conducted at Mr. G. Tye's this evening.

August 10th, 1867.

Cranbrook Penny Bank would seem to have achieved some success. This second notice is dated nine years after the initial opening of the service.

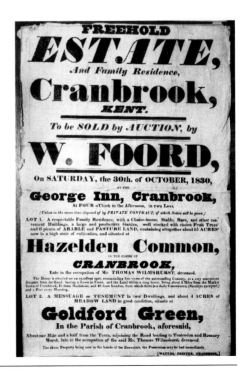

A notice advertising the sale of two properties belonging to the late Mr Thomas Wilmshurst, one at Hazelden Common and the other at Goldford Green. The sale was to take place at The George Inn on 30 October 1830, and the name of the auctioneer was W. Foord.

A centenary service took place at Providence chapel, Cranbrook on 18 June 1903. This chapel was an early type of prefabricated building. Made in London, it was transported to its present site by horse and wagon.

Mr G. Hatcher at the stables behind the bakers shop, which subsequently became Chaneys.

A team of four oxen from Sissinghurst Castle parade in Cranbrook's first horse show, *c*. 1912. This show ran for a number of years from 1912–32. At one time Cranbrook had a charter for two fairs a year and a weekly market which lasted until the last century. Horse trading was also a regular feature and Mr Farley, Curator of Cranbrook Museum, and some of the more senior residents of the town remember seeing horses 'showing their paces' in Jockey Lane.

The corner of Stone Street and Waterloo Road with Mr G. Curl going to Fryer's dairy for milk in January 1912.

The old forge may be seen on the left of The Hill, *c.* 1905, in front of the sign 'S. Stokes'. Beyond may be seen 'The Crane' coffee tavern. The water-cart has obviously just passed along the street leaving a clean strip in the middle of the road.

Going for water from the Tanyard pump, *c.* 1900.

St David's bridge earlier this century, with the tower of the church of St Dunstan clearly visible.

St David's bridge, *c.* 1910. The River Crane, never more than a stream, ran under the bridge, through a tunnel under the road. In the background may be seen the tower of St Dunstan's church.

Cranbrook School, *c*. 1938. In 1518 John Blubery bequeathed his 'chief mansion place in Cranbrooke' to found the school and for over 450 years it has occupied the same site. In 1574 Queen Elizabeth I granted the school its royal charter, and it became known as 'The Free Grammar School of Queen Elizabeth in Cranbrook'. Blubery's mansion disappeared in 1727 but School House was built on the same site, and this remains the centre of the school today. The ancient parish church of St Dunstan is prominent in the centre background. The school has close links with the church and surrounding town.

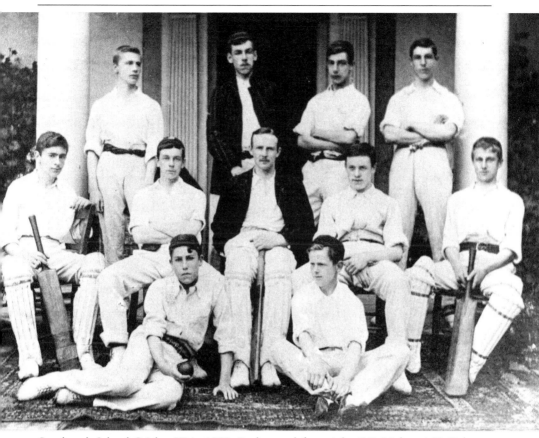

Cranbrook School Cricket XI in 1898. Back row, left to right: F.B. Nolan, A.T. Colman, D.A. Jones, C.B. ? – it is impossible to decipher the name of this last player. Second row: G.L. Robathan, J.K. Armstrong, F.N. Gammidge (captain), S.M.T. Burpitt, A.E. Prosser. Front row: F.W. Faithfull, P.C. Stokes. It is interesting to note that several of the school team have moustaches.

Cranbrook School 1st XV, 1943. The captain at this time was C.M.A. Vallance (front row, centre). On his right is T.E.N. Hart, who loaned this photograph and a year later captained Crowden House Cricket XI.

Mr W. Cooper was a sportsman and local hero to many boys. He played for Cranbrook Town Football Club. Today this picture and the many medals he won are displayed in Cranbrook Museum. The team is pictured having won the Weald of Kent League. Mr Cooper is seated on the second row, second on the right.

Union mill at Cranbrook is one of the most impressive of the smock mills still standing. It was constructed in 1814 for Henry Dobell and modernized in 1840. At that time it was powered only by the wind, but a steam engine was installed in the 1860s. Milling of flour ceased some years ago but the mill is still in full mechanical order and produces grain for livestock. Much of the restoration of this magnificent mill was carried out by Mr John Russell, whose family owned the mill from 1832. Kent County Council, in order to preserve this monument, underwrote certain of the outstanding costs. The figure in the doorway may be the miller.

The mill-pond, Cranbrook. During the sixteenth century the whole Weald became a rural workshop and mill-ponds became a very valuable commodity.

Glassenbury House, *c.* 1910. Dating back to 1473, the present mansion was built by Walter Roberts and the house remained in the hands of the Roberts family until a few years ago. It is believed that the name is derived from the Saxon idiom of 'inis witrin' meaning a watery or glassy place. The house is surrounded by a moat and stands in a large timbered park. 'Jaffa', one of the chargers which Napoleon rode at the Battle of Waterloo, is reputed to be buried in the grounds. Jane Roberts inherited the house and estate on the death of her mother in 1971 but when she married two years later the couple decided to move into the coach-house. Glassenbury House went on the market, thus ending its long association with the Roberts family.

Oxen from Glassenbury outside the old post office, *c.* 1900. The building in the centre of the picture is reputed to be a former police station situated on The Hill.

SECTION FIVE

Rural Areas

The county library van, c. 1925. By 1925 Kent County Council had increased its library centres to such an extent that it became impossible to supply them with books. Where consignments of books had previously been sent by rail and carrier, now it became necessary to obtain a vehicle in order to make these deliveries. The first lorry used for this specific purpose was a 30 cwt Vulcan and it carried 2,000 books. A Thorneycroft lorry was subsequently purchased, capable of carrying nearly 200,000 volumes to various centres in the county. It was the policy of K.C.C. that rural areas were the first to be supplied with books. Centres were originally set up in schools but, later, village halls or institutes were used for this purpose.

The Green, Benenden, early this century.

Benenden from the post office, *c*. 1905. Benenden is perhaps best known today for its girls school, one of its former pupils being the Princess Royal. Much of the village was developed by Lord Cranbrook in the last century.

All Saints' church, Biddenden, *c.* 1895.

Edward III was responsible for inviting skilled weavers from the continent to Kent, thereby leading to the great cloth-making industry of the Weald which prospered from this influx of foreign workers. Wool was readily available from the Kentish flocks and two other important commodities, water power and fuller's earth, were also available for finishing the cloth. Most of the clothiers worked on a fairly small scale at, for example, the Clothworkers Hall, Biddenden, where it is believed that some of the required buying and selling also took place.

The Street, Benenden, in 1890. In Charles Igglesden's book, *A Saunter Through Kent With Pen and Pencil,* we are told of an extraordinary feat which took place in 1839. Mr Thomas Hopper, who stood 6 ft high and possessed great strength, was a farmer and grocer and his corner shop occupied the site near the enclosure which formed the angle between the two streets. Having successfully cleared every turnpike gate between Maidstone and Tenterden, he undertook, for a wager of £10, to run half-a-mile in two minutes. Despite a near collapse within 15 yd of the winning post he ultimately won his wager. Subsequently 'he was conveyed to bed almost in a delirious state through the terrific exertions he had undergone, but recovered a short time afterwards.' A stone was erected in his memory in Biddenden churchyard, following his death, aged 70, in 1867.

The Street at Biddenden. This scene is remarkably similar to the photograph opposite, except for the fact that motor cars have taken the place of the many pedestrians standing outside The Red Lion Inn.

Hendon Hall, Biddenden, *c.* 1910. The iron ore of the Weald has been worked and smelted since the days of the Romans, and evidence of the industry is apparent in such names as Hammer Pond, Furnace Lane and Blower's Cottage. A certain amount of wealth was generated, leading to the construction of large residences such as Hendon Hall at Biddenden, built in the eighteenth century.

Mr Harry Witherden wearing a smock, pictured earlier this century. He was the uncle of Mr 'George' Weaver, a well-known resident of Tenterden.

The Biddenden Maids were born joined together by the hips and shoulders in about 1100. They lived together in the above state for thirty-four years, until one of them was taken ill and died. The surviving twin was advised to be separated from the body of her deceased sister by dissection, but she refused the separation by saying these words, 'As we came together we will also go together.' Within six hours she also died. They bequeathed to the churchwardens of the 'Parish of Biddenden and their successors, certain Pieces or Parcels of Land in the Parish, containing Twenty Acres'. Hasted, in 1790, discredits the traditional origin and believed that the twenty acres of land, known as 'Bread and Cheese Land', was given by persons unknown, the yearly rents to be distributed among the poor of the parish. Cakes (stamped with the portrait of the 'Biddenden Maids'), bread and cheese were distributed to the poor of the parish for over 800 years.

Bread and cheese was formerly distributed at Easter to the poor of the parish from this residence known variously as Old Maids House, or the Old Parish House, Biddenden. Strangers in the area were given a bread roll in memory of the 'Biddenden Maids'.

The Old Parish House, Biddenden, *c*. 1900.

Sandhurst village, *c*. 1909. Before the advent of aerial photography, long-range views were often taken from the top of the church tower or from a commanding hill. The clock tower, windmill and a number of hop-oasts are clearly visible in this picture.

Sandhurst Green, with its pleasant row of weather-boarded cottages and large memorial dominating the scene. This monument was erected 'in 1883 in grateful memory of Arthur Oakes, Esq., J.P., by Parishioners and friends of Downgate in this Parish'. This clock tower, which must have been a boon to the villagers, stands just behind the later war memorial which was apparently erected in Mr Jempson's garden!

The Mill, Sandhurst, c. 1903. On the left hand side of the cart is a whetstone, normally seen in farmyards and used for sharpening agricultural implements, while Sandhurst mill with its impressive five sweeps stands in the background. A pencilled note on the back of this postcard, sent in 1903, tells us: 'Mr Jempson in garden where War Memorial now is.'

Sandhurst mill, c. 1890, was the only one in Kent to have five sweeps. The first reference to milling was in the thirteenth century but the practice ceased here early this century.

SECTION SIX
Rolvenden

St Mary's church, Rolvenden, *c.* 1905. This church has a history going back to the thirteenth century, while the nave may be traced to the fourteenth century. Much additional work was carried out during the last century including the removal of the box pews and galleries in 1898. They were subsequently made into choir stalls and pews by the then vicar the Revd Percival Smith and a team of willing helpers. The first mention of a permanent settlement in the area was in the fifth century, and it is claimed that many of the village sites and the various names found there are of Saxon origin.

The Gate House, Rolvenden, *c.* 1910. The Gate House was formerly known as Frensham Manor and is one of the oldest houses in the parish. It was completely restored during the latter years of the 1920s and subsequently became known by its original name – Frensham Manor. Notice the hop-oasts in the background, testifying to the fact that this was a hop-growing area.

Rolvenden Layne village store, *c.* 1910. Rolvenden Layne is a little hamlet close to Rolvenden. The village store sold a wide variety of goods as the sign states. It was also the post office and a meeting-place for many of the villagers, some of whom are seen here with the proprietor. During the store's long history it was sometimes known as 'The Layne Corner Shop'.

Mrs Amy Wilson driving her cart past The Ewe and Lamb public house during Rolvenden's Jubilee procession. Her daughter Margaret is a passenger. The carnival procession was one of the highlights of Rolvenden's Jubilee day programme and it is believed that over 300 people took part in the fancy dress parade.

A typical Kentish farm wagon outside The Bull, *c.* 1905.

The blacksmith standing outside the forge in Rolvenden Lane, *c.* 1920. Most of the small towns and villages had their own forge which would have been kept busy with a variety of work including shoeing the many horses used on the farms in the surrounding country-side.

Belgian wounded recouperating outside Rolvenden Church Room, c. 1915. The men were apparently nursed here by members of the Voluntary Aid Department. It is believed that the matron in charge was Mrs Coombe Baker, seen wearing the darker coloured uniform. The building subsequently became the village hall.

The 'Dunce Dance' performed by Rolvenden children earlier this century. Unfortunately it has been impossible to discover any further details about this amusing incident.

SECTION SEVEN
Tenterden

Tenterden has a long and interesting history. As early as 1449/50 the town joined the Confederation of the Cinque Ports as a 'limb' of Rye. The five Cinque Ports and the 'two Antient Towns' (Rye and Winchelsea) had undertaken to supply a certain number of manned and equipped ships for the King's service. Rye, at this time, was unable to meet its quota and turned to its more wealthy neighbour, Tenterden, for assistance. An elaborate agreement called 'The Composition between Rye and Tenterden' was drawn up in 1493 which specified each town's relative position and privileges. However, over the years disputes arose and these continued into the eighteenth century. Originally Tenterden had a bailiff as chief citizen, but subsequently this office was raised to that of mayor. In 1600 Tenterden was granted a new charter and John Hales who was then bailiff became the town's first mayor. The above picture is of the second mayoral seal of the seventeenth century and depicts a three-masted ship under full sail, denoting the town's early connection with the sea.

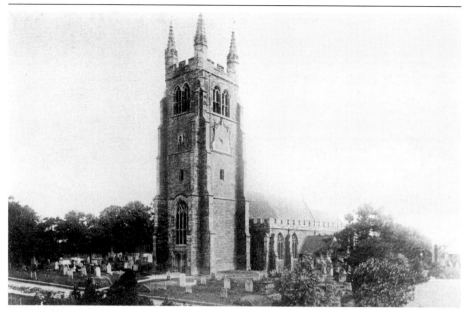

St Mildred's church, Tenterden, *c.* 1880, showing the old clock face. A new clock was installed on the occasion of Queen Victoria's Jubilee (see pp. 152–3). The pair of double doors on the west side of the tower are unusual; there is only one other church in Kent with similar ones. An early vicar of St Mildred's was married to Horatia, the daughter of Nelson and Emma Hamilton, and it is recorded that 'they were happy in the town where they were shown much kindness by the people.'

The interior of St Mildred's church, Tenterden, *c.* 1910. Built in the twelfth century, the church was named after St Mildred, Abbess of Minister-in-Thanet, who died in the eighth century. The church has seen many changes including the removal of the galleries and box pews in 1864.

Before the advent of aerial photography views taken from church towers were much in demand. This one shows the High Street looking towards West Cross, around 1920.

The High Street, *c.* 1865. On the left is the old thatched barn which belonged to Pittlesden Manor and next to it the premises of the Tenterden Fire Brigade. This single-storey building was erected in 1823 and demolished in 1972. In the distance may be seen the old tollgate which was removed in the 1880s (see p. 130).

The High Street, Tenterden, *c.* 1890, where annual sheep and cattle fairs were held on the greens beneath the trees for nearly seven hundred years. The stock fairs were ultimately removed to Corporation Field at East Cross, thus alleviating much of the hardship experienced by the residents of the High Street who had suffered constantly from the dirt and flies during these fairs.

Tenterden May Fair, *c.* 1890. This fair was originally held in the High Street and many of the local townsfolk complained of the smell and noise occasioned by so many cattle and sheep being confined in such a small area. The fair, one of the oldest in the county, was held on 2 May. A large number of beasts were sold, the number quoted ranging from 12,000 to 15,000 sheep and 1,500 head of cattle. These figures, however, would have referred to the fair when it moved to its site in Glebe Field.

The High Street, Tenterden. The buildings on the north side of the street date mainly from the eighteenth century. The road was constructed in 1762 and originally had a turnpike, while the fine trees bordering both sides were planted in 1871.

Tenterden's Fire Brigade, *c.* 1905. Tenterden's horse-drawn fire engine is outside the old station which stood in the High Street, opposite the Vine Inn on the corner.

Tenterden Town Hall, pre-1912, before the addition of the attractive balcony.

A meet of the local hunt, a popular sight with the inhabitants of Tenterden, passing the Town Hall on the left, *c.* 1920.

The mayoral procession of 1920. The First and Second Sergeants at Mace, Stephen Goodsall and Nelson Tickner, precede the mayor, Alderman Edgar Howard, who was made a baron at the coronation of George V. Stephen Goodsall had already completed fifty-three years service with Tenterden Corporation.

Tenterden Town station building, *c.* 1910. The station was erected in 1903 and the Kent and East Sussex Railway completed in stages between 1900 and 1905. The line became a casualty of the Beeching 'axe', closing to traffic in 1961. However, a group of enthusiastic people have worked to re-open part of the route (from Tenterden Town to Northiam station) and this has become a popular tourist attraction.

This vehicle carried a maximum of six passengers and operated for the Rother Valley Railway. It operated in the area surrounding Tenterden Town station. The driver is Frank Clarke.

The old toll-gate, High Street, *c.* 1875. The large Italianate building which subsequently became the National Westminster Bank looked most incongruous and dominated the surrounding properties when erected in the middle of the nineteenth century. This view looks west along the High Street.

Penderel Court, *c.* 1910. Penderel Court, on the extreme left of this photograph, was formerly Penderel School, a small private establishment which ran for over fifty years. The headmistress, Miss Lizzie May McCowan Hall, served for more than thirty years and was a popular figure in and around Tenterden.

Children dressed in the fashion of the day in Tenterden High Street, *c.* 1900. The two girls on the left have wooden hoops, which were a popular toy with youngsters earlier this century when the streets were relatively free from traffic. The small boy, front centre, has an iron hoop. Today these playthings are unlikely to be seen outside museums.

St Benedict's Priory, *c.* 1900. This Tudor-style building was also known by the name of Finchden Manor after the family who owned it in earlier times. It has had a varied history. It was leased to the Benedictine monks from 1876 and they used it as a seminary for a number of years. Mr George Lyward founded a home for emotionally disturbed boys at the priory in 1935 and during the Second World War it was requisitioned by the Army. After the war it continued as a home for many young boys. Following Mr Lyward's death in 1973 the house was sold to pay death duties.

The sign denoting the 'Soup Kitchen' of 1875 is inscribed over the door of a small brick building subsequently used as a workshop. The distribution of soup became necessary due to the agricultural depression during the latter half of the nineteenth century when many people suffered great hardship and near starvation. The country was ordering imported wheat from America to overcome the shortage at home, caused in many instances by poor harvests. Earlier in the century William Cobbett in his *Rural Rides* painted a picture of deplorable distress in country places, with local banks being forced to close.

The High Street, earlier this century, looking towards East Cross. Stephen Hook, butcher, ran his business from the fifteenth-century black and white building which was originally a 'hall-house' but altered the following century. Many early photographs show this shop with joints of meat hanging outside.

Mr Hook and his staff, Christmas 1902. The business was carried on from the family home in the High Street behind which were open fields, where cattle were fattened, and a slaughter-house.

A peaceful scene early this century showing Tenterden mill-pond. Much of the prosperity of these early towns depended on their water supply when fulling mills were driven by water power.

The horse-trough and one of the town pumps earlier this century. St Mildred's church tower is just visible behind the trees.

The High Street, Tenterden, looking east, earlier this century under a deep blanket of snow. The building on the extreme right is the Zion Baptist chapel, erected in 1835 and renovated in 1887. The Tudor cottages behind the telegraph pole were unfortunately demolished and a modern bank erected in their place. The next building is The White Lion, an old coaching inn. In *The Pictorial Record* of 1899 it was stated that: 'The house contains 18 bedrooms, commercial room, coffee and smoke rooms, billiard room, private and saloon bars, and a large banqueting room, 50 ft long by 20 ft wide, where dinners are given and meetings held. . . . Needless to say the cuisine is irreproachable, and the wines, spirits and ales, cigars, etc., sold of the very best quality; while visitors will find the ability to hire post horses and carriages here a great convenience.' The tall building beside it was erected in 1780 by Dr John Mace. It is known today as The Pebbles, part of it housing Tenterden library.

It has been impossible to confirm whether this was an outing to the coast organized for the employees of Lewis and Hyland together with their wives and families as we suspect, but all the passengers look as if they intend to enjoy their trip.

One of the earliest of the coach builders to operate in Tenterden was H.F. Goldsmith, who advertised his work in building and restoring carriages in Thomson's Directory of 1890. Mr W.T. Mercer erected the above premises, around 1900. Carriages were constructed in the smith's shop on the ground floor, which was separate from the body-making and wheel shops, while the paint shop was on the upper level. The vehicles were winched up an incline to this second floor which was kept at an even temperature and free from dust.

Consignments of hides arriving at Tenterden tannery in Smallhythe Road. Earlier this century many small towns had their own tanneries, hides being collected from around the country. Some of the residents of Tenterden were less than happy at the smell from the tannery which permeated the town, but others considered it to be health-giving!

Bells Lane, *c.* 1910. Tenterden's theatre was built here in the eighteenth century. Early in the nineteenth century the area had a bad reputation for fights between families living in over-crowded conditions. Today it is best remembered for the happier times, and many of the cottages have names relating to the theatre, such as Playwrights Cottage and Theatre Cottage.

The Gibbet (farm), *c.* 1907, when demolition work was being carried out among the farm buildings. It included the destruction of two oast-houses.

A favourite form of transport for the ladies was a pony and trap. The long whip is an interesting feature, the length necessary in order to reach the horse. Unfortunately it has been impossible to identify the driver.

The last time the large family of Mr and Mrs Body of The Gibbet were all together was on 2 March 1907, when this photograph was taken. With seven boys and six girls this was a happy occasion. Various spouses were also present together with their offspring. Back row, left to right: Arthur, Charles, Mildred, Ed, Hilda, Thomas, William and Geoffrey. Second row: Queenie, Harold, Olive, William, Sarah (née Upton), Margaret. Front row: Dorothy, Dick (standing), Biddy (the baby), Margery, Margaret (standing), Bertha. Mr R. Body, who lent this photograph and identified his many relatives, is the small boy standing in the front on the left.

Two children, believed to be Bertha and Margery Body, play in the 'Hangman's tree', so called as it was thought to stand on the site of the old gibbet. The last execution that took place in Tenterden was in 1785 when two men were hanged at Gallows Green for burglary. Mr R. Body, whose grandfather lived and farmed at The Gibbet during the first twenty years of this century, believes that the hangings would have taken place nearer the cross-roads and not on this farm despite its name.

With thirteen children in William and Sarah Body's family it is impossible to say who the baby is occupying this very elaborate pram.

Arthur Body, seen here as a private in the 2nd Battalion (Weald of Kent) Buffs.

Bertha Body, back row, third from left, and other VADs from the Tenterden division in 1913.

Three Tenterden cyclists, who may have operated for the postal service, *c.* 1880. With the invention of the bicycle or, as the early ones were known, velocipede, many public services and tradesmen took delivery of them. They were also used by certain branches of the military, while postal and police units were also formed.

A cycling club assembled by the gatehouse to Heronden Hall, West Cross, *c.* 1900. These clubs were popular with members of both sexes and flourished at a time when the roads were less congested than they are today. Despite the dust, members were quite happy to travel long distances on less than perfect machines and over fairly rough surfaces. The cycling boom reached its peak in the 1890s and many clubs sprang into being. Most of the early ones, however, were 'men only'.

Waterloo Day parade, *c.* 1910, passing the decorated Town Hall. A contingent from the Buffs, the Royal East Kent Regiment, is headed by members of the local fire brigade, followed by the town band. The occasion was obviously a happy one judging by the number of interested spectators.

Tenterden High Street, *c.* 1950. Sheep have played a vital part in the economy of the county of Kent and flocks were a common sight in the streets of Tenterden. On the right is the Town Hall, adjoining The Woolpack Inn. The former was built in 1790 to replace the original hall which was destroyed by fire in 1661. The graceful ironwork balcony was added in 1912.

Among the seven windmills in the Tenterden area was Pinyon's, which was demolished in December 1912 because the structure had become unsafe. The frame of the mill was toppled by a wire rope attached to a traction engine. All that remained after the event were the two massive wheels.

Throwing Pinyon's mill, December 1912.

Leigh Green mill, Appledore Road, *c.* 1910. The smock mill, sometimes known as Pilbeams after Mr J. Pilbeam who bought it in 1887, was destroyed by a horrendous fire which swept through the building on 26 November 1913. All that remained of the structure may be seen below. Local residents said that the mill was working at 10 p.m. and well alight an hour later. Older residents had looked on the mill as a landmark as it could be seen over a wide area.

An advertisement from Thomson's Directory and Almanac 1905 relating to the well-known store of H. Boorman & Co. There were other branches in the area including one at Rolvenden and another at Benenden. Samuel Boorman founded the business in 1819. The shops sold a wide variety of goods including groceries and provisions, clothes for all age groups, house furnishings and boots and shoes.

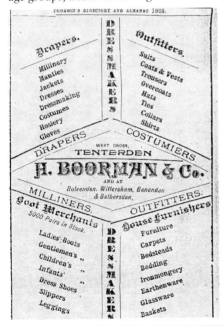

East Cross, Tenterden, *c.* 1900. Most of the shops have canopies jutting over the street, which may have given a certain amount of shade to pedestrians on hot days as well as protecting perishable goods from the rays of the sun.

Golden Cross, Tenterden early this century. At one time the small building on the right hand side was The Plough beerhouse.

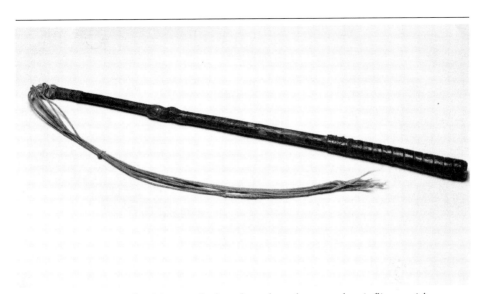

This scourge in Tenterden Museum is thought to have been used to inflict punishment on William Smith who, in 1778, was indicted for petty larceny. Pleading guilty he was publicly whipped until his back bled. In 1752 two men were tied to the tailgate of a cart and whipped for stealing geese, and in 1760 a female 'cheat' was ordered to be whipped as part of her punishment.

This Farman bi-plane was first observed flying above Reading Street while taking part in the Europe Air Race from Calais to Hendon and back, *c.* 1911. Unfortunately the pilot, M. Renaux, was forced to make an emergency landing on Romney Marsh and the grounded plane became an object of great curiosity to the many spectators who came from afar to view it.

Mr E.J. Haffenden denouncing tithe at the fifth distraint sale on his farm, *c.* 1910.

The Grange at St Michaels was purchased by Mr H.F. Varley and run as a small modern preparatory school called 'Asheton'. Pupils at the school wore distinctive red blazers and were a familiar sight in and around Tenterden. The school closed in 1930.

The British School, Ashford Road, *c*. 1925. From 1820 the Dissenters had their own Sunday school, founded to give a basic but free education to children from poorer families. In 1838 a schoolroom was added to the rear of the meeting-house and then a purpose-built school was erected in Ashford Road. It became known as the 'British School', the pupils of which seem very interested in the photographer.

A ceremony outside the Jireh Strict Baptist chapel, *c.* 1920. Although a well attended event, it has been impossible to identify this religious occasion.

An engraving, *c.* 1820, of the High Street with the church of St Mildred. The clock was removed during the reign of Queen Victoria and a new one erected to celebrate her Golden Jubilee. However, many of the residents preferred the former, more distinctive clock face, shown here, to the later one.

Celebrations in Tenterden High Street on the occasion of the Diamond Jubilee of Queen Victoria. Note the new clock face on the church tower.

St Michaels village in 1900 before it became a suburb of Tenterden. In the distance is the village church which was erected by public subscription.

St Michaels, a suburb of Tenterden, *c*. 1890. St Michaels was a completely rural area consisting of a few cottages without a church or school until early n the 1860s. Originally it was known as Boresisle.

The Crown Inn, St Michaels, *c.* 1910. The inn was owned by Ashford Breweries as the sign denotes. Note the three different types of transport.

The Cottingham family outside their forge in Ashford Road, St Michaels, *c.* 1935. Most of these villages were completely self-sufficient with their local stores, wheelwrights and forges. St Michaels would have served a wide rural community at this time.

The ferrygate at Smallhythe at the turn of the century. On the right hand side of the road is Smallhythe Place, originally the residence of the port officer and for twenty-nine years the residence of the popular stage actress Dame Ellen Terry.

Smallhythe Place and ferrygate in 1900.

Dame Ellen Terry, *c.* 1920. Dame Terry, the famous actress of the last century, first set-tled in Winchelsea before moving to Smallhythe Place. She occupied the house for twenty-nine years until her death in 1928. She is best known for her long association with Sir Henry Irving which lasted for over thirty years.

Priest's House, Smallhythe, 1890. Today Smallhythe is a quiet backwater rather than a thriving port. The road leads to Romney Marsh which may be seen in the distance.

Wm. BODY & SONS,

Potmon's Heath Wharf,

WITTERSHAM and High Street, TENTERDEN.

Tenterden, Rolvenden, Northiam and

Bodiam Railway Wharves.

COAL AND COKE MERCHANTS,

Bricks, Tiles and Drain Pipes, Lime Sand, Beach and Rock.

All kinds of AGRICULTURAL SEEDS.

Special Quotation for Coal by Truck.

Cattle Feeding Cakes and Artificial Manures.

An advertisement relating to 'Wm. Body & Sons' of Potmon's Heath Wharf from Thomson's Directory and Almanac of 1904 (see opposite).

Mr W. Body's barge at Smallhythe, 1905. Mr W.S. Body of The Gibbet had a difficult job in finding suitable employment for his seven sons. He invested in two barges which plied between Potmon's Heath Wharf and Rolvenden Wharf at Witterham Road, usually bringing coal and building materials up river and taking corn down. This barge, seen here at Smallhythe Dock, is loaded with beech. Mr W.S. Body is seen on the right hand side of the photograph, either overseeing the operation or merely being an interested spectator!

Acknowledgements and Bibliography

I am deeply grateful for all the help from the many people who so freely gave of their time and knowledge in the preparation of this book:

Mr Leonard Pierce, secretary of the Goudhurst and Kilndown Local History Society and to that organization for the loan of many of the photographs relating to Goudhurst; Mrs J. Porter of Hope Mill, Goudhurst; Mr Lewis Waghorn, usually known as 'Wag', local historian of Hawkhurst, who so kindly put his own personal collection at my disposal; Mr R. Body of Hope Farm, Snarden, who allowed me to use many photographs from his family albums; Mr F. Farley, Curator of Cranbrook Museum, who permitted my photographer, Mr Peter Greenhalf, to reproduce many of the pictures of the area held by the museum; Cranbrook Local History Society; Mr Peter Allen of Cranbrook School; Mr Paul Dean, also of Cranbrook, for the loan of his photographs; Mr Ted Hart, an ex-pupil of Cranbrook School; Mrs Denise Barr and Brenchley and Matfield Local History Society; Maidstone Museum and Art Gallery; Dr Burgess, Curator of Tenterden Museum; Tenterden Local History Society for the loan of their material; Mr J. Weaver, usually known as 'George' of Tenterden; Weavers Library for the use of their collection; Miss Jane Starling of Tenterden Library; Mrs Linda Robart of Ashford Library

Finally I would like to thank my photographer, Mr Peter Greenhalf, who worked at times under tremendous pressure and never let me down. I should like to record that this book has only been made possible by the assistance I have received from all the above.

Books I have found useful in the compilation of this volume include:

Reminiscences of Old Cranbrook, Joe Woodcock; *Goudhurst & Kilndown Parish Past*, Gordon W. Batchelor; *Hawkhurst Remembered*, Lewis H. Waghorn; *Tenterden* and *Tenterden in Times Past*, R.S. Spelling; *Bygone Tenterden*, Aylwin Guilmant; *A History of Kent*, Frank W. Jessup.